20
Rebus Mini-Books
FOR
Emergent Readers

by Carol Pugliano-Martin

SCHOLASTIC
PROFESSIONAL BOOKS

New York • Toronto • London • Auckland • Sydney
Mexico City • New Delhi • Hong Kong • Buenos Aires

To Baxter and Hayden—mini-books for my mini-men

Cover design by Norma Ortiz

Cover and interior artwork by Jane Dippold and Susan Calitri

Interior design by Sydney Wright

ISBN: 0-590-51327-3

Contents

Introduction

Welcome to *20 Rebus Mini-Books for Emergent Readers*, a collection of rhymes and verse that is sure to set your students on the journey toward independent reading! On a variety of topics complementing favorite themes, these easy-to-make mini-books include beloved nursery rhymes and fresh, predictable verse. Designed to instill in young readers the confidence essential to becoming successful readers, each mini-book helps students learn to read new words and build important reading skills. These rebus mini-books provide the following features and benefits:

◎ Reading mini-books helps students learn the conventions of print, such as directionality (left to right, up to down, front to back), an important first step in learning to read.

◎ The rebus format encourages young readers to pay close attention to the text, prompting children to think about what they are reading by asking such questions as "What could make sense here?" This use of context clues is one of the strategies reflective readers use as they read.

◎ Fun-to-read rebus illustrations help to convey the idea that symbols (letters and pictures) stand for sounds and words.

If your classroom is filled with children of varying abilities, as most classrooms are, then the mini-books in this book will be a helpful resource. Use them however they fit your instructional needs. Invite beginning readers to simply fill in the picture "words" as you read the printed text, and challenge more experienced readers to read both the words and the pictures.

To enhance learning with these books, you may wish to try one or all of the following activities with your students:

◎ Consider teaching younger children with the Favorite Nursery Rhymes first to build their confidence in reading through familiar stories and tales. Here, they'll gain firsthand experience with contractions like *couldn't* and *he's*. While young readers may not be familiar with reading contractions, they are likely to have encountered them in oral language and will know their meaning. Invite children to look for contractions within the text. Discuss reasons why authors might use them in their writing. Then, invite your students to read the fresh, new tales in Classroom-Perfect Verse. Their positive experiences with the well-known tales will help spur them on to tackle new reading challenges.

◎ Have students form a sentence with the rebus illustrations and words from one or more of the mini-books. You can do this by having the children hold cards with the pictures or words, or wear the cards around their necks. After the sentence "team" has lined up in front of the class, have the rest of the class read the sentence out loud together. Take this activity further by inviting students to create their very own rebus story or sentence by directing a sentence team.

◎ Display many different words and pictures on a table. Ask students to put together a sentence using the words and illustrations, checking first to make sure that sentences can be readily constructed. Students may work in groups, in pairs, or alone. Encourage students to share their sentences with the rest of the class.

◎ Choose a group of children to represent one of the stories, with one child for each word or picture. As in the other activities, have students line up in their proper order. (It's extra challenging and a more valuable learning experience if the children organize themselves independently.) The students representing words hold their word cards. The children representing pictures act out their word instead of holding a picture. With the picture words displayed nearby, invite students in the audience to find the picture word cards and hand them to the students who acted out those pictures.

◎ Ask students to draw/write their own rebus stories. As with reading the mini-books, this activity will familiarize children with the directionality of print and give them experience with writing. Invite each child to read his or her story aloud to the class. Imagine the satisfaction children will feel when they get to be authors!

◎ Pair up less experienced readers with those who have more skills. Have the pairs read the books together, with the less experienced reader reading the pictures and the more experienced reader reading the words. This can be a wonderful experience for both sets of students—the early readers learning that they may look to their peers for help and the more experienced readers feeling empowered as teachers.

◎ Tuck a set of rebus mini-books in your classroom library for students to reread and rediscover. Emergent readers will love reading all 20 of these irresistible mini-books again and again. You can also send them home for children to share and read with families and friends.

I wish you and your students success and fun in beginning your reading adventures together!

Assembling the Mini-Books

Begin by making copies of the mini-book you would like to use. Keeping the pages faceup, invert every other page. Place the pages in your photocopier and make one double-sided copy of the mini-book for each student.

After constructing a few mini-books as a class activity, your students are sure to enjoy making them on their own and reading the mini-books they've created. Introduce the bookmaking process by showing your students what they'll be expected to do—from folding and matching up the pages to stapling and coloring. Demonstrate and discuss each of the steps.

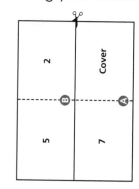

1. Cut the pages in half along the solid line.

2. Put the pages in order.
   For an 8-page book, place page A faceup on top of page B.

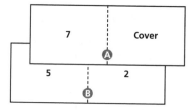

   For a 12-page book, place page A faceup on top of page B. Then place page B faceup on top of page C.

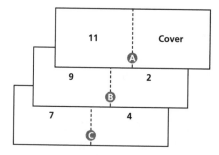

3. Fold the pages in half along the dotted line, making a little book.

4. Check to be sure that all of the pages are in sequence. Then, staple them together along the spine.

5. Once the mini-book is assembled, it's time to invite your students to color the rebus pictures and read the mini-book!

How I wonder
what you are!

Twinkle, Twinkle Little Star

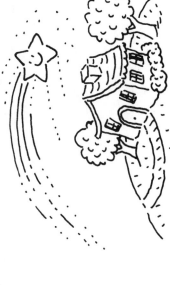

Twinkle, twinkle

little

Key

 star

 world

 diamond

 sky

Up above the
so high,

Like a

in the

Twinkle, twinkle
little

How I wonder
what you are!

The

Hey, Diddle, Diddle

The little laughed

to see such sport,

Key

 cat

 fiddle

 cow

 moon

 dog

 dish

 spoon

3

and the

1

Hey, diddle, diddle!

4

The jumped over the

6

And the ran away with the .

Was a merry old soul,

Old King Cole

He called for his

Key

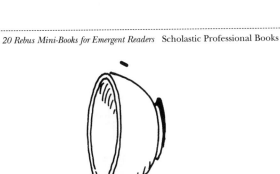 king

 bowl

 pipe

 fiddlers

And a merry old soul

was he.

He called for his ,

Old Cole

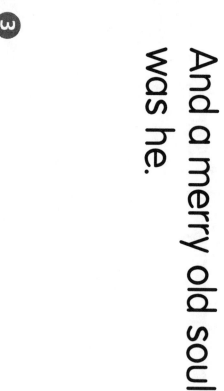

And he called for

his  three.

1

3

4

6

Humpty Dumpty

sat on a

And all the 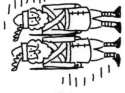's

Key

 Humpty Dumpty

 king

 horses

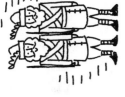 men

 wall

Couldn't put
together again.

20 Rebus Mini-Books for Emergent Readers   Scholastic Professional Books

had a great fall.

All the

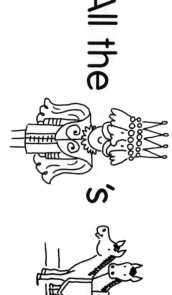

's

's man!

Pat-a-Cake

And put it in the

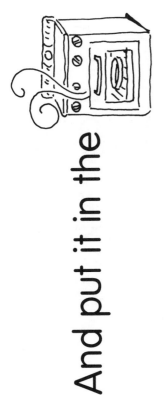

5

Key

 cake

 oven

 baker

 baby

7

Pat-a-

pat-a-

Bake me a

As fast as you can.

Pat it and prick it,

And mark it with a B

For   and me.

Buckle my ⬚ .

2

One, Two, Buckle My Shoe

Seven, eight,
Lay them straight.

5

Key

shoe

sticks

door

hen

7

One, two,

Three, four,
Knock at the
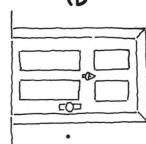
.

Five, six,
Pick up

.

Nine, ten,
A big fat

.

Come blow your  !

Little Boy Blue

20 Rebus Mini-Books for Emergent Readers Scholastic Professional Books

Where's the little  that
looks after the  ?

Key

 boy

 cow

 horn

 haystack

sheep

corn

Little 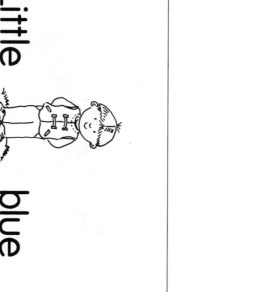 blue

The 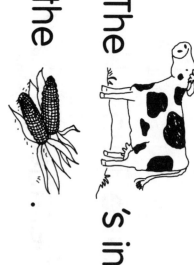 's in the meadow,

He's under the fast asleep.

The 's in the .

He caught the ,

He caught the .

5

B

He swam in a ,

And climbed on the .

2

Key

 turtle

 puddle

 mosquito

 minnow

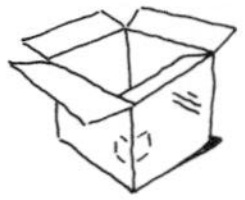 box

 rocks

 flea

7

There Was a Little Turtle

A

He snapped at a

He snapped at a 🐛.

He snapped at a 🐟

And he snapped at me.

There was a little 🐢

Who lived in a .

He caught the 🐟

But he didn't catch me!

Time to play with  .

Time for School

Time to swing on  .

Isn't it great?

Key

crayons    smocks

blocks    swings

books    school

Time to draw with

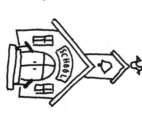

.

Time to read new

,

It's time for

And I can't wait!

And wear our paint

.

Page 2

I see a

Down on the farm.

Down on the Farm

Page 5

I see a

Down on the farm.

Key

 sheep

 horse

 cow

 pig

 chicken

I see a

Down on the farm.

And woolly white

Down on the farm.

I see a

Down on the farm.

I love to be

Down on the farm.

20 Rebus Mini-Books for Emergent Readers Scholastic Professional Books

Trees

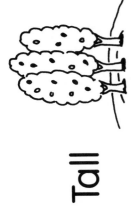

Tall

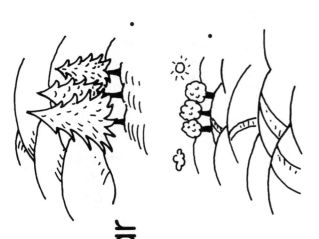

Near

Far

Key

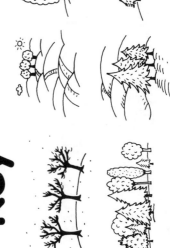

trees

leaves

Small .

Bright

in the fall .

Winter bare .

High up in the

air .

I'm so glad there

are 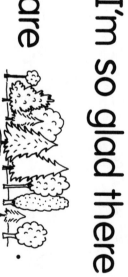.

Who lived in my 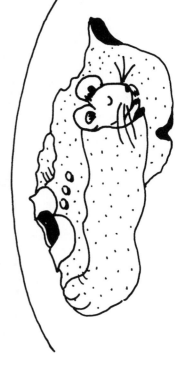 .

2

B

The Mouse

A

So I said he could stay.

5

Key

 house

mouse

blouse

7

3

He stayed in my closet

Inside my blue

He would not go away.

4

1

There once was a

That  in my

Cozy in my blue  .

6

Make them into  .

Peanut Butter and Jelly

20 Rebus Mini-Books for Emergent Readers Scholastic Professional Books

---

Take some  .

Make it into .

Key

 peanuts

 peanut butter

 grapes

jelly

grain

bread

sandwich

Take some

.

Take some

.

Make them into

.

Eat your

and

And you will be well fed!

The  is cool.

20 Rebus Mini-Books for Emergent Readers Scholastic Professional Books

Weather

It stings my

Key

 sun

 snow

 rain

 face

 wind

 sled

The is hot.

When I walk to school.

The

blows my hair

The

is cold.

when I ride my

all over the place!

2

My  helps me smell.

All About Me

A

5

My help me run.

7

Key

book

nose

 eyes

hands

legs

My help me see.

My help me touch.

This is a that is all about me.

And now this about me is done.

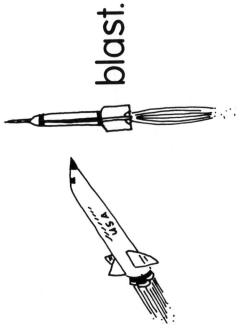

go choo-choo!

2

blast.

5

Things That Go

A

Key

 cars    boats

 trains   rockets

 airplanes   bicycle

7

1

go zoom zoom zoom!

3

so blue.

fly in the sky

And when I'm on
my
I go very fast!

float.

6

4

Spring is a time for .

20 Rebus Mini-Books for Emergent Readers Scholastic Professional Books

Spring

Spring is a time for .

Key

flowers

rain

birds

grass

lambs

chicks

hands

Spring is a time

for 🐦 🐦

to fly home again.

Spring is a time

for green 🌱 .

Spring is a time

for 🌸 .

Spring is time

for fluffy 🐤 🐤

sitting in my 🖐️ .

Sat on a

Freddy the Frog

Who was
wearing a

Key

 pig

 wig

frog

 log

Freddy the

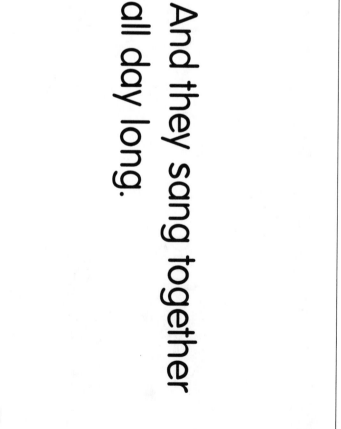

Croaking out a song.

And they sang together
all day long.

Along came a

 on the ground.

Garden Friends

A

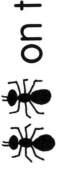 on the tree.

Key

 ladybugs    spiders

 ants    beetles

 bees    fireflies

 flowers

Buzzing all around.

in the

in the bushes.

1

in the garden.

Pretty as can be!

light up the sky

6

D is for  .

E is for  .

I can say the alphabet all by myself!

Alphabet Fun

20 Rebus Mini-Books for Emergent Readers Scholastic Professional Books

X is for  .

Y is for  .

Z is for  .

who is having a snack.

Key

 nuts   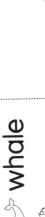 rhinoceros

 ostrich   :☼: sun

 peach    turtle

 queen   umbrella

 violin

 whale

 x-ray

yak

zebra

F is for .

G is for .

H is for
who loves to laugh.

A is for .

B is for .

C is for
with soft white hair.

U is for .

V is for .

W is for
with a very big grin.

Key

 apple

 bear

 cat

 dog

 elf

 frog

giraffe

hyena

 ice cream

 jar

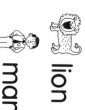 kangaroo

 lion

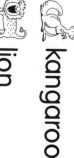 man

I is for .

J is for .

K is for driving a car.

20 Rebus Mini-Books for Emergent Readers Scholastic Professional Books

R is for .

S is for .

T is for who cannot run.

L is for

M is for .

N is for

in a big tin can.

20 Rebus Mini-Books for Emergent Readers Scholastic Professional Books

O is for

P is for .

Q is for

sitting on the beach.